Food Field Trips

Let's Explore
Beans!

Jill Colella

Lerner Publications ◆ Minneapolis

Hello Friends,

Everybody eats, even from birth. This is why learning about food is important. Making the right choices about what to eat begins with knowing more about food. Food literacy helps us to be more curious about food and adventurous about what we eat. In short, it helps us discover how delicious the world of food can be.

Did you know that beans are superfoods? Superfoods give our bodies lots of vitamins and minerals. Want a lot of energy? Eat your beans—in tacos, soups, or even tasty veggie burgers. You'll feel energized like a superhero!

For more inspiration, ideas, and recipes, visit www.teachkidstocook.com.

Jill

About the Author
Happy cook, reformed picky eater, and long-time classroom teacher, Jill Colella founded both *Ingredient* and *Butternut*, award-winning children's magazines that promote food literacy.

Lerner Publications Company
An imprint of Lerner Publishing Group, Inc.
241 First Avenue North
Minneapolis, MN 55401 USA

For reading levels and more information, look up this title at www.lernerbooks.com.

Main body text set in Mikado
Typeface provided by HVD

Library of Congress Cataloging-in-Publication Data
Names: Colella, Jill, author.
Title: Let's explore beans! / Jill Colella.
Description: Minneapolis : Lerner Publications, 2020. | Series: Food field trips | Includes bibliographical references and index. | Audience: Ages 4–8 | Audience: Grades K–1 | Summary: "Beans are packed with nutrition and found in cuisines around the world. See how beans grow, meet the farmers who grow them, and engage in two activities: making bean dip and growing a bean plant." – Provided by publisher.
Identifiers: LCCN 2019045820 (print) | LCCN 2019045821 (ebook) | ISBN 9781541590342 (library binding) | ISBN 9781728402802 (paperback) | ISBN 9781728400174 (ebook)
Subjects: LCSH: Cooking (Beans)—Juvenile literature. | Beans—Juvenile literature. | LCGFT: Cookbooks.
Classification: LCC TX803.B4 C56 2020 (print) | LCC TX803.B4 (ebook) | DDC 641.6/565—dc23

LC record available at https://lccn.loc.gov/2019045820
LC ebook record available at https://lccn.loc.gov/2019045821

Manufactured in the United States of America
1 – CG – 7/15/20

SCAN FOR BONUS CONTENT!

Table of Contents

Picture Glossary

flowers

pods

roots

seeds

sprout

ALL ABOUT BEANS

Beans are part of the legume family.
Legumes are plants that grow pods.

Seeds grow in the pods.
These seeds are beans.

5

LET'S COMPARE

There are many kinds of beans.
Beans can be light or dark.

Some are round and others flat. Some have spots and stripes!

LET'S EXPLORE

Beans grow in fields. They start as tiny seeds in soil.

What other foods grow in fields?

The seeds need water and sunshine to sprout.

LET'S GROW BEANS

A bean plant starts to grow from a seed. The stem grows upward. Roots grow down into the soil.

Soon the plant makes flowers.

11

Pods begin to form. Inside a pod are tiny seeds.

Can you see the seeds?

Do the pods look fuzzy or smooth?

Some bean plants grow tall.
Others grow wide.

Bean pods grow about as thick as a pencil. Some grow thicker!

Do these pods look ready to be picked?

Green beans are also called string beans. Do you see the tiny strings on the ends?

When we eat green beans,
we eat the whole pods.

With other beans, we only eat the seeds inside the pods.

We cook beans in boiling water. Then they are ready to eat!

Do you have a favorite dish with beans?

LET'S COOK

Always have an adult present when working in the kitchen!

POWER-PACKED BEAN DIP

INGREDIENTS

- 1 15-ounce can (425 g) garbanzo beans, or chickpeas (white beans work too)

- 1 clove garlic, crushed

- 2 teaspoons ground cumin

- ½ teaspoon salt

- 1 tablespoon lemon juice

- 2 teaspoons olive oil

- snacks for dipping, such as carrots, pretzels, or tortilla chips

1. Drain the liquid from the can of garbanzo beans into a bowl. Set the bowl aside.

2. Combine the beans, garlic, cumin, salt, lemon juice, and olive oil in a blender or food processor.

3. Blend the ingredients on low speed. Gradually add the saved bean liquid until the dip is smooth.

4. Scoop the dip into a serving bowl and enjoy it with snacks!

SEE THIS RECIPE IN ACTION!

LET'S MAKE

GROW YOUR OWN BEAN PLANT

MATERIALS

- dry lima beans (two per plant)
- bowl
- water
- clear plastic cup
- potting soil
- spray bottle

1. Let the beans soak in a bowl of water overnight.

2. Loosely fill the cup two-thirds full with potting soil.

3. Use your finger to make a hole in the soil. Place two beans in the hole, then cover them with soil.

4. Moisten the soil with water from the spray bottle.

5. Place your cup on a sunny windowsill. Spray gently with water when the soil looks dry. Watch as your plant grows!

Let's Read

ChooseMyPlate—Vegetable Group Food Gallery
https://www.choosemyplate.gov/eathealthy/vegetables/vegetable-group-food-gallery

Dunn, Mary R. *A Bean's Life Cycle*. North Mankato, MN: Capstone Press, 2018.

Education.com—Create a Bean Mosaic!
https://www.education.com/activity/article/Create_Lasting_Mosaic/

Jenkins, Martin. *Caterpillar and Bean*. Somerville, MA: Candlewick Press, 2019.

Play Ideas—25 Bean Crafts for Kids
http://www.playideas.com/25-bean-crafts-for-kids/

Rattini, Kristin Baird. *Seed to Plant*. Washington, DC: National Geographic, 2014.

Index

Photo Acknowledgments

The images in this book are used with the permission of: © Alex Liew/iStockphoto, p. 15 (picking beans); © ALLEKO/iStockphoto, p. 19 (beans in sauce); © BogWan/iStockphoto, pp. 3 (germination), 10; © Brycia James/iStockphoto, p. 17; © CasarsaGuru/iStockphoto, p. 9 (planting); © DS70/iStockphoto, pp. 3 (soybean pods), 5 (soybean pods); © fcafotodigital/iStockphoto, p. 6 (black beans); © FotografiaBasica/iStockphoto, p. 6 (jars of beans); © FSTOPLIGHT/iStockphoto, p. 6; © Fudio/iStockphoto, p. 4; © Gajus/iStockphoto, p. 7 (hands holding beans); © GANCINO/iStockphoto, p. 5 (beans in bags); © ghornephoto/iStockphoto, p. 8; © Goddard_Photography/iStockphoto, p. 12; © Janine Lamontagne/iStockphoto, p. 1; © Kateryna_Mostova/iStockphoto, p. 19; © ksushachmeister/iStockphoto, p. 22 (beans in water); © ktaylorg/iStockphoto, p. 5; © LazingBee/iStockphoto, pp. 3 (Borlotto beans), 7 (Borlotto beans); © Liudmyla Liudmyla/iStockphoto, p. 11; © Luis_Nogueira_Damas/iStockphoto, p. 22; © Magdalena Kleemann/iStockphoto, p. 18; © MargoeEdwards/iStockphoto, p. 20; © Mathia Coco/iStockphoto, p. 16; © mtreasure/iStockphoto, p. 14 (climbing beans); © Natalie Ruffing/iStockphoto, p. 15 (purple beans); © Opla/iStockphoto, pp. 3, 9, 23; © oticki/iStockphoto, p. 14; © pashapixel/iStockphoto, p. 7; © photohampster/iStockphoto, pp. 3 (black and white flowers), 11 (black and white flowers); © robynmac/iStockphoto, p. 21; © stevanovicigor/iStockphoto, p. 9 (row of soybeans); © stockcam/iStockphoto, p. 11 (red flower); © tab1962/iStockphoto, p. 15; © Zoya2222/iStockphoto, p. 13.

Cover Photos: © DEBOVE SOPHIE/iStockphoto (girl in garden); © Janine Lamontagne/iStockphoto (various legumes); © Karisssa/iStockphoto (bowl of cooked beans); © Magdalena Kleemann/iStockphoto; © Natalie Ruffing/iStockphoto (purple beans)